Easy Password Tracker

Site	Username	Password

I0455322

Easy Password Tracker

Site	Username	Password

Easy Password Tracker

Site	Username	Password

Easy Password Tracker

Site	Username	Password

Easy Password Tracker

Site	Username	Password

Easy Password Tracker

Site	Username	Password

Easy Password Tracker

Site	Username	Password

Easy Password Tracker

Site	Username	Password

Easy Password Tracker

Site	Username	Password

Easy Password Tracker

Site	Username	Password

Easy Password Tracker

Site	Username	Password

Easy Password Tracker

Site	Username	Password

Easy Password Tracker

Site	Username	Password

Easy Password Tracker

Site	Username	Password

Easy Password Tracker

Site	Username	Password

Easy Password Tracker

Site	Username	Password

Easy Password Tracker

Site	Username	Password

Easy Password Tracker

Site	Username	Password

Easy Password Tracker

Site	Username	Password

Easy Password Tracker

Site	Username	Password

Easy Password Tracker

Site	Username	Password

Easy Password Tracker

Site	Username	Password

Easy Password Tracker

Site	Username	Password

Easy Password Tracker

Site	Username	Password

Easy Password Tracker

Site	Username	Password

Easy Password Tracker

Site	Username	Password

Easy Password Tracker

Site	Username	Password

Easy Password Tracker

Site	Username	Password

Easy Password Tracker

Site	Username	Password

Easy Password Tracker

Site	Username	Password

Easy Password Tracker

Site	Username	Password

Easy Password Tracker

Site	Username	Password

Easy Password Tracker

Site	Username	Password

Easy Password Tracker

Site	Username	Password

Easy Password Tracker

Site	Username	Password

Easy Password Tracker

Site	Username	Password

Easy Password Tracker

Site	Username	Password

Easy Password Tracker

Site	Username	Password

Easy Password Tracker

Site	Username	Password

Easy Password Tracker

Site	Username	Password

Easy Password Tracker

Site	Username	Password

Easy Password Tracker

Site	Username	Password

Easy Password Tracker

Site	Username	Password

Easy Password Tracker

Site	Username	Password

Easy Password Tracker

Site	Username	Password

Easy Password Tracker

Site	Username	Password

Easy Password Tracker

Site	Username	Password

Easy Password Tracker

Site	Username	Password

Easy Password Tracker

Site	Username	Password

Easy Password Tracker

Site	Username	Password

Easy Password Tracker

Site	Username	Password

Easy Password Tracker

Site	Username	Password

Easy Password Tracker

Site	Username	Password

Easy Password Tracker

Site	Username	Password

Easy Password Tracker

Site	Username	Password

Easy Password Tracker

Site	Username	Password

Easy Password Tracker

Site	Username	Password

Easy Password Tracker

Site	Username	Password

Easy Password Tracker

Site	Username	Password

Easy Password Tracker

Site	Username	Password

www.ingramcontent.com/pod-product-compliance
Lightning Source LLC
Chambersburg PA
CBHW060340290526
45793CB00003B/680
9781445780108